Sunlit Zone

John Woodward

Heinemann Library
Chicago, Illinois

Consultant: Lundie Spence, Ph.D.
Director, SouthEast Center for Ocean Sciences Education Excellence, South Carolina Sea Grant Consortium

Produced by The Brown Reference Group plc
Project Editor: Tim Harris
Sub Editor: Tom Webber
Designer: Jeni Child
Picture Researcher: Sean Hannaway
Illustrator: Mark Walker
Managing Editor: Bridget Giles

Printed in China by WKT Company Limited

08 07 06 05 04
10 9 8 7 6 5 4 3 2 1

Library of Congress Cataloging-in-Publication data
Woodward, John, 1954-
  Sunlit zone / John Woodward.
    v. cm. -- (Exploring the oceans)
Includes bibliographical references and index.
Contents: The sunlit zone -- Your mission -- A coral reef -- Down the reef slope -- A coral bloom -- An artificial reef -- Hidden life -- Swimming with a sea giant -- Flying with fish -- Shark attack! -- A cool ocean current -- Feeding frenzy -- Water and weather -- The weedy Sargasso Sea -- Exploring the Gulf Stream -- Rich fishing -- Whale watch -- A red tide -- The frozen ocean -- Diving with seals -- Mission debriefing.
  ISBN 1-4034-5127-3 (hardcover) -- ISBN 1-4034-5133-8 (pbk.)
1. Marine ecology--Juvenile literature. 2. Oceanography--Juvenile literature. [1. Marine ecology. 2. Ecology. 3. Oceanography.] I. Title.

QH541.5.S3W67 2004
551.46--dc22
                                2003021268

Acknowledgements

The author and publishers are grateful to the following for permission to reproduce copyright material:
Front Cover: Coral groupers on the Great Barrier Reef, Australia. (Reinhard Dirsherl, Ecoscene). Back Cover: Corbis: Mark A. Johnson
p.1 Ron and Valerie Taylor/Ardea; p.2t Stuart Westmorland/Corbis; p. 2c Howard Hall/Oxford Scientific Films; p.2b Jim Zuckerman/Corbis; p.3 Georgette Douwma/Photodisc, Inc.; p.4 Ken Usami/Photodisc, Inc.; pp.6–7 Stephen Frink/Corbis; p.7 Tim Wright/Corbis; pp.8–9 Karen Gowlett-Holmes/Oxford Scientific Films; p.10 Ian Cartwright/Photodisc. Inc.; pp.10–11 Georgette Douwma/Photodisc, Inc.; p.12 Soames Summerhays/Natural Visions; pp.12–13 Robert Garvey/Corbis; pp.14–15 Robert Yin/Corbis; p.15 Doc White/Ardea; p.16 NOAA; pp.16–17 Jim Zuckerman/Corbis; p.18 Heather Angel/Natural Visions; pp.18–19 Ron and Valerie Taylor/Ardea; pp.20–21 Howard Hall/Oxford Scientific Films; p.21 Mark Deeble & Valerie Stone/Oxford Scientific Films; pp.22–23 ANT Photo Library/NHPA; p.23 Jeffrey L. Rotman/Corbis; pp.24–25 Stuart Westmorland/Corbis; p.25 Image Quest 3-D/NHPA; pp.26–27 Ron and Valerie Taylor/Ardea; p.27 NOAA; p.28 Vaisala Oy; p.29 Jacques Descloitres/NASA/GSFC; pp.31–31 Norbert Wu/NHPA; p.32 Ron and Valerie Taylor/Ardea; pp.32–33 Rodger Jackman/Oxford Scientific Films; pp.34–35 Bill Coster/NHPA; p.35 Jack Fields/Corbis; pp.36–37 Francois Gohier/Ardea; p.38 Pete Atkinson/NHPA; p.39 Karen Gowlett-Holmes/Oxford Scientific Films; pp.40–41 Dr. Eckhart Pott/NHPA; pp.42–43 Heather Angel/Natural Visions; p.43 Kurt Amsler/Ardea; p.44 Image Quest 3-D/NHPA.

Some words are shown in bold, **like this.** You can find out what they mean by looking in the glossary.

Contents

The Sunlit Zone

This colorful lionfish is one of many animals that live in the sunlit zone.

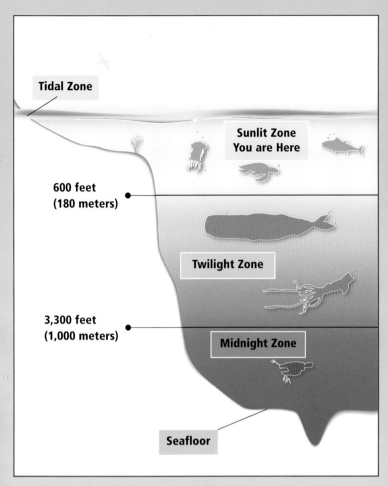

Tidal Zone

**Sunlit Zone
You are Here**

**600 feet
(180 meters)**

Twilight Zone

**3,300 feet
(1,000 meters)**

Midnight Zone

Seafloor

oceans affect the weather and **climate.** You will discover what lives in them, and where. You will see amazing creatures and plants. Some will be the biggest, strangest, most deadly, and most beautiful animals on the planet.

The sunlit zone

Your journey starts in the water at the top of the ocean. This area is called the sunlit zone. This zone extends down about 600 feet (180 meters) below the surface. The water in this layer is bright and warm, especially near the **equator.**

Sunlight can shine through water, because water is clear like glass. This is important because ocean life needs the light and heat of the Sun, just as animals and plants on land do. There is a lot of light a few feet below the surface. In the deeper water, it is darker because less light is getting through. This is like shining a light through a thin piece of glass and a very thick piece of glass.

The light is also a different color. Sunlight includes all the colors of the rainbow. Shallow water **absorbs** the red and yellow light first. Only the blue light reaches as deep as the bottom of the sunlit zone, at 600 feet (180 meters).

It is easy to explore the sunlit zone because you can see where you are going. And there is a lot to see. Most of the animals in the ocean live there.

The oceans of the world are huge and mysterious. People cross them all the time in ships, but few people have explored far below the waves. It is difficult work. People cannot breathe underwater. They need special equipment just to look below the surface. Deep below the surface, they need to be protected from the ice-cold water and crushing **water pressure.** Exploring the oceans is as difficult as exploring space. People now know more about the surface of the moon than they do about the deep seas.

You can go along with scientists who are trying to find out more about the oceans. You will get all the equipment you need for this mission. You will study how the

Your Mission

Clouds of life

In some parts of the ocean, the water is very clear. Even 150 feet (46 meters) below the surface, you can still see bright colors. But in other regions, the water is full of tiny living **organisms.** These creatures are too small to see without a **microscope.** They make the water cloudy. This keeps much of the sunlight from shining through. So, the sunlit zone in these regions is much shallower than usual.

You are going to start your journey in the warmest, brightest blue ocean waters on Earth. These are the **tropical** coral seas. You will dive down to explore **coral reefs.** In other areas, you will find out how corals and other animals turn shipwrecks into underwater gardens.

Your mission will then take you far out into the tropical ocean. You will see the fish and seabirds that feed there. You will come face to face with one of Earth's biggest **predators.**

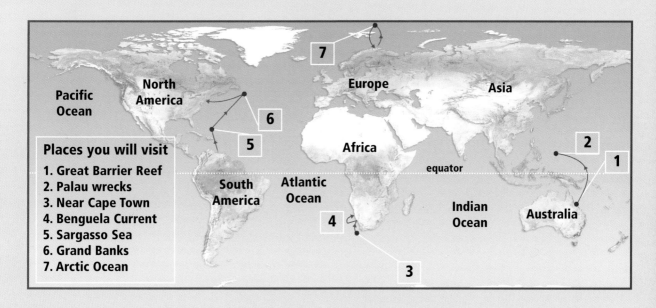

Places you will visit
1. Great Barrier Reef
2. Palau wrecks
3. Near Cape Town
4. Benguela Current
5. Sargasso Sea
6. Grand Banks
7. Arctic Ocean

You will soon discover that ocean waters do not stand still. Instead, they flow around the world in massive swirling **currents.** You will explore one of these ocean currents. You will see how it affects life in the ocean. It even affects the animals and people who live on shore.

A tropical coral reef is an amazing place to visit. Corals are many shapes and colors.

Then, you will travel north into the cold waters of the North Atlantic. These waters have a lot of food. You will dive with huge whales as they round up large schools of fish and eat them. You will find out why the oceans of the North Atlantic can support so many fish.

Finally, you will explore the frozen world of the Arctic. You can even dive under the **sea ice** of the Arctic Ocean to see what lives there. Your journey will take you from the warm seas of the tropics to the ice of the Arctic Ocean.

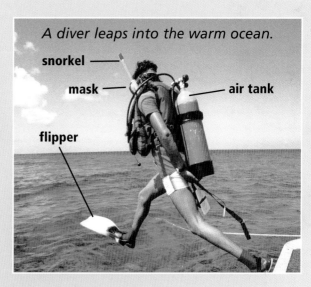

A diver leaps into the warm ocean.

snorkel

mask

air tank

flipper

A Coral Reef

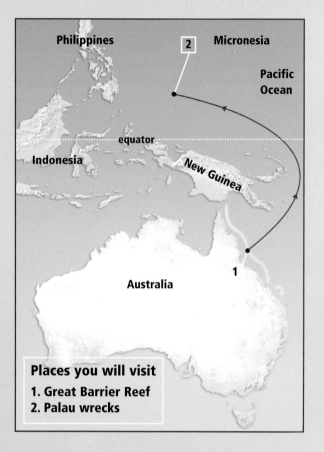

Places you will visit
1. Great Barrier Reef
2. Palau wrecks

is so big it can even be seen from space! The Great Barrier Reef is not one reef but a collection of more than 2,500 separate reefs. Each reef has been created by millions of corals. Corals are animals that look like small sea anemones. Corals do not live by themselves but instead form huge **colonies.** Each coral is attached to its neighbors. Corals are supported by skeletons made of chalky calcium carbonate (a chemical found in **limestone** rock). Over many years, layer on layer of corals have grown on the skeletons of dead corals. Gradually, great chalky reefs have been created, covered with a layer of living corals.

Your journey starts near the Great Barrier Reef off the northeast coast of Australia. It is early morning, and you are about to look more closely at the reef. The sky is brilliant blue, and the water is crystal clear. You carry your equipment across the bright, silvery sand to a boat, then load up and set off.

The Great Barrier Reef is the biggest **coral reef** in the world. It is more than 1,250 miles (2,300 kilometers) long. That is longer than the coastline of California. The reef

Wearing just a swimsuit, mask, and flippers, you slip over the side of the boat. Attached to the mask is a snorkel, a bent tube that sticks out of the water and allows you to breathe. You swim slowly over the top of the reef, looking down at the fantastic shapes of the corals. They glow different colors in the sunlight—blue, purple, yellow, and pink—like a very colorful underwater garden.

In a way, that is exactly what a coral reef is. Tiny, plantlike living things called **algae** live in each coral. They are so small that there may be 2 million algae living in an area of coral as big as your fingernail.

Algae can make sugar from water and carbon dioxide gas dissolved in the water. This process is called **photosynthesis.** But coral algae can only photosynthesize if there is sunlight. The corals use some of the sugar to build their own bodies. In return they give the algae vital **nutrients** and a safe place to live. When different types of **organisms** do things that help each other, it is called a mutualism.

Pygmy seahorses live on coral reefs, such as the Great Barrier Reef off the northeast coast of Australia. Although pygmy seahorses do not look like fish, that is what they are.

Down the Reef Slope

Back in the boat, you head out to the edge of the reef. You are going to dive down the outer reef slope, using **scuba** equipment. You put the scuba suit on, check your air supply, and drop into the water.

The reef is alive with fish swimming over the corals. **Coral reefs** have more different types of fish than anywhere else in the ocean. Groups, or shoals, of brilliant green puller fish swim by. Tiny purple damselfish and yellow butterfly fish look for food among the corals. Plump parrotfish crunch bits off the corals. These fish use tough teeth to do this. Big fish, such as groupers, watch the smaller fish. They are hoping for an easy meal. Shoals of sweetlip fish swim past quickly. They are big colorful fish that eat small **organisms** floating in the water.

There are plenty of other animals besides fish. There are colorful sea slugs, delicate prawns, which look like large shrimp, and spiny sea urchins. There are also spiky crown-of-thorns starfish. These are not fish at all.

Scuba gear

If you swim just under the water surface, you can use a snorkel. But for a deeper dive you must use scuba gear. Scuba stands for Self-Contained Underwater Breathing Apparatus. The tanks on your back carry enough air for you to stay underwater for several minutes.

They are sea stars, and they eat corals. Very large sea snails like the giant triton eat the crown-of-thorns starfish. The connection between **predators** and prey is called a **food chain.**

Diving deeper

As you dive down the reef slope, the water becomes less bright. The corals down here grow much more slowly than the corals near the surface. That is because their **algae** receive less light and cannot make as much food. But the slow-growing corals have stronger skeletons than those higher up. Chunks of coral from higher up often get broken off by storm waves. They tumble down the reef slope.

Using a tool called a core sampler, you drill into the reef to take a sample of the rock. It has layers, like the growth rings in timber. This is because the rate at which coral reefs grow varies over the year.

Named for their big lips, these sweetlips suck small animals from the ocean near coral reefs.

A Coral Bloom

You have timed your visit to the Great Barrier Reef very well. It is November, which is spring in Australia. Now is a good time to see how corals reproduce, or create new corals. Corals can reproduce in two ways. Each one can grow buds that turn into new corals, so eventually there are hundreds of corals. But each new coral is a **clone.** That means each one has the same set of **genes.** If one gene has a problem or is damaged, all the corals have the same problem. The other way new corals are made is by spawning. That is when the corals release **eggs** or **sperm.** The eggs and sperm join to make a new coral. This new coral has a different mix of genes from any other coral. On the Great Barrier Reef spawning happens in November, a few nights after the full moon.

Corals cannot move, so they simply release all their eggs or sperm into the water. All the corals of the same species do this on the same night. This makes sure that the eggs of one coral get the chance to fuse with the sperm of another coral. This is called fertilization.

Mass spawning

Your driver takes the boat out over the reef just as the moon rises. You are wearing your **scuba** gear and a helmet with a built-in headlamp. Above the reef, you switch on your headlamp and slip over the side into the water. Everywhere you look, tiny pink beads are rising through the water. They are eggs and sperm that have been released by the corals below. The eggs released by one coral are then ready to fuse with the sperm of another coral. Each fertilized egg develops into a new coral.

A single coral is called a polyp. This pink polyp has just let go of a tiny egg. The egg floats upward. It might be fertilized by sperm from another coral.

Return to the surface

Soon there are so many coral eggs and sperm in the water that you cannot see your way. But you thought of this before setting off, and attached yourself to the boat with a rope. You pull yourself back, climb on the boat, and head for the beach.

Next morning, you discover that the water in the reef **lagoon** is colored pink with billions of fertilized coral eggs. It is the same all along the reef, as far as you can see. Up and down the whole length of the Great Barrier Reef, all the corals of the same species have spawned. And over the next few nights, all the other species of corals will spawn, too.

On the Great Barrier Reef thousands of corals release their eggs and sperm on one night in November.

An Artificial Reef

Many islands in the southwestern Pacific Ocean have **coral reefs** around them. Some of the most colorful reefs surround the Rock Islands of Palau, in Micronesia. About 60 years ago, this was the place where a fierce World War II (1939–1945) battle was fought. Many Japanese ships were sunk by American forces. The wrecks of the ships still lie on the seabed among the islands. This seafloor is within the sunlit zone.

Your next dive is to take a look at the Palau wrecks. But do not expect them to be as they were when they sank. Since then, all kinds of corals and other

sea creatures have begun living on and inside the wrecks. The ships have become human-made reefs. You are going to find out how much coral can grow in 60 years.

A sunken giant

Your first target is the *Iro Maru*. This is a huge ship that lies on the bottom of a **lagoon.** The deck is 70–90 feet (21–27 meters) below the surface. That's as deep as two houses are high. The *Iro Maru* was sunk by a torpedo in 1944. Near the front of the ship you see a huge hole where the torpedo exploded. As you look at the wreck, you see that corals are growing on the rusty metal.

A wreck for a home

You return to the surface, then travel to another lagoon and dive again. This time you visit the wreck of the Chuyo Maru (below), a cargo ship that was sunk by the American submarine USS Sailfish on December 4, 1943. This wreck is covered with black corals, which have very hard skeletons. These corals have also become a home for many lionfish.

You have to be very careful, though. It is easy to damage corals. You would not want to do that. You measure the corals with your waterproof tape measure. Some are much bigger than others, even though they probably all started growing at the same time. Some of the branching corals are very large. They can grow more than the length of your hand in a single year.

These curved and branching corals are growing on a wrecked Japanese warship in the sunlit zone near Palau.

Hidden Life

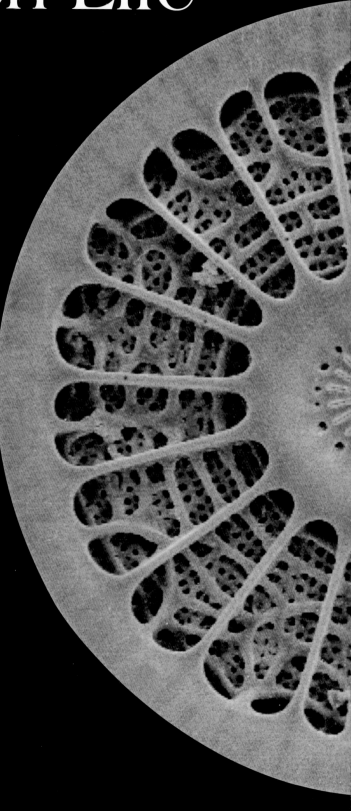

The boat takes you to a much larger research ship called *Neptune*. It has a well-equipped laboratory. You are going to dive again, but this time you will look for life in a different area of sea.

The ocean to the east of Palau is clear and dark blue. Compared to the **coral reefs** around the islands, the ocean seems lifeless. There are no colorful shoals of fish. The seafloor is very deep. It is more than two and a half miles (four kilometers) below the surface, and light cannot shine that deep. So there is no coral.

You decide to take samples of the ocean water from different depths and look at it more closely. Using a **microscope,** you examine water taken from the sunlit zone

Research ships

Ocean research ships, like the one below, have laboratories on board. There, scientists can look at water samples to see what lives in the ocean. They use powerful microscopes so they can see even tiny **organisms.**

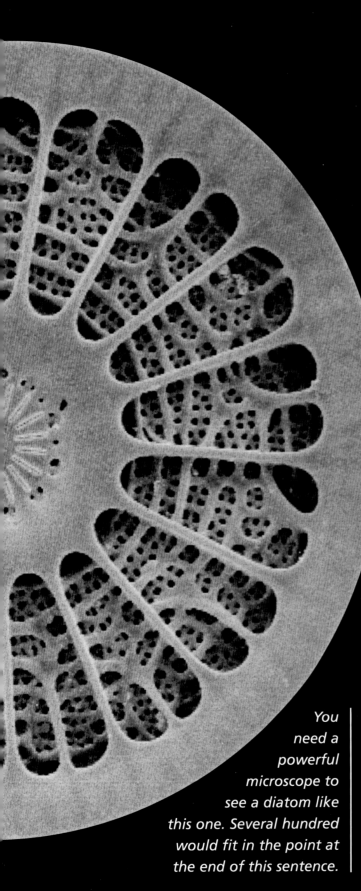

and water from much deeper in the ocean. There is little in the water from very deep, but the water sample from the sunlit zone contains tiny see-through animals. Some look like shrimp. Others do not look like anything you have seen before.

Scattered among the animals are even stranger, smaller objects. Some are like glass seashells. Others are like see-through jewels or spiky balls. They do not look alive. They are not moving like the animals.

A world of tiny animals

You check out the pictures of tiny **organisms** in the books on the ship. The books help you discover that the organisms are tiny **algae.** The algae are related to the ones that live in corals. Some are called diatoms. Like those in the corals, they can use sunlight to make food. Algae are eaten by the tiny animals you have seen through the microscope. The tiny animals are mostly baby crabs, sea urchins, and clams. They all drift near the surface of the ocean in a living layer called **plankton.**

Fishing with a net

On the way back to Palau, you decide to see how much plankton there is in the water. You trail a net with very fine mesh over the side of the boat. When you haul in the net, there is not much in it. The reason is that plankton is scarce in most clear **tropical** oceans. You try again closer to the shore and find more plankton. There are also more fish closer to the shore. Fish like places where there is plenty of plankton for them to eat.

You need a powerful microscope to see a diatom like this one. Several hundred would fit in the point at the end of this sentence.

Swimming with a Sea Giant

Your samples show that some parts of the ocean contain more **plankton** than other parts. There is always more plankton near the sunlit surface, and there seems to be more near the coast. And where there is **microscopic** plankton, there are bigger animals. Some of these drift along in the water, so they are part of the plankton, too. But others are active swimmers that live among the plankton because it is the most abundant source of food in the open ocean.

Your next job is to find out why the plankton is so important. So you set off again in the *Neptune*, watching for any signs of plankton-rich water. You want to know if it can be found away from the

coast. After an hour at sea you spot a few seabirds diving into the sea. You decide to take a much closer look.

Super shark

The birds are catching small fish, which are feeding in an area where there is a lot of plankton. Wearing your **scuba** gear, you slip over the side of the boat to see what is in the water. Most of the plankton is too small to see, but there are also jellyfish and strange see-through creatures called comb jellies.

The comb jellies flash with glittering rainbow colors. You dive down to take a closer look. All of a sudden, a big shadow moves overhead. It is a massive whale shark. It is the biggest fish in the sea, and it has

A siphonophore floats through the sunlit zone in search of shrimp and fish to eat.

a huge gaping mouth! Relax. The shark is not interested in you. It has very small teeth and feeds on plankton and small fish. The shark swims through the swarms of tiny creatures with its mouth wide open to feed. The water flows into its mouth and out of the **gill** openings behind its head. On the way the water passes through gills, which filter out the plankton.

A whale shark can grow to more than 40 feet (12 meters) long and weigh 12 tons (12,200 kilograms) or more. That is as long as a school bus and

as heavy as two elephants! The whale shark gets that big by eating things that are mostly much smaller than itself. This shows just how much **plankton** is drifting about near the surface of the sunlit zone.

Although a whale shark has a very large mouth, its teeth are tiny. It does not need large teeth because the food it eats is so small the shark can swallow it whole.

Flying with Fish

You look over over the ocean through your binoculars. Binoculars allow you to watch things that are too far away for a good view with just your eyes. You see a big black bird with long wings. It is swooping down to the ocean surface and snatching something up in its beak. It is a frigatebird. You would like to take a closer look, but the bird is flying fast. Luckily your research ship has a speedboat hooked to the back. So you ask someone to drive you and follow the action.

While your boat speeds across the waves, you see the frigatebird swoop down again. It seems to catch a fish in midair. As you get closer, you see that fish are leaping out of the water and gliding on extra-long fins. They are flying fish. They are leaping out of the water to escape from bigger fish that are attacking them from below.

The motor of the speedboat scares the flying fish even more. Suddenly, the ocean is covered with them. Each one flies just above the surface. The fish keep the lower part of their tail in the water and beat it madly to build up speed. The fish move amazingly fast. Your speedboat is already traveling at 37 miles (60 kilometers) per hour, and the fish are still getting away from you.

Suddenly, a flying fish drops into the boat. It was probably dropped by a frigatebird and is quite dead. You take it back with you to the research ship and discover that its mouth is filled with **plankton.** So flying fish are plankton eaters, just like the giant whale shark.

On the way back, you get a major fright. A huge black creature leaps out of the water ahead of you. Then it falls back with a great splash. It is a manta ray. Rays are flat fish. They seem to fly through the water on broad fins that look like wings. The manta ray is the biggest ray, with a wingspan of 12 feet (4 meters). That is as wide as a car is long. The ray looks scary, but it is another plankton eater and is not at all dangerous to people.

A diver looks very small as she swims after a huge manta ray.

A flying fish is very streamlined.

Streamlining

Water is a very dense, thick substance. So, moving through water is much more difficult than moving through air. If you have ever tried to walk quickly in a swimming pool, you will know all about it. Ocean animals that need to move fast, such as many fish, have a sleek, pointed shape that slips through the water very easily. This type of shape is described as streamlined. Some very fast fish, such as marlin, have even better streamlining than a jet plane has.

Shark Attack!

Places you will visit
1. Near Cape Town
2. Benguela Current

Namibia

2

Benguela Current

South Africa

Benguela Current

● Cape Town

1

Cape Town on the southern tip of Africa. Here the sharks prey on the **colonies** of Cape fur seals that breed on small islands off the coast.

Sharks are not just awesome killers. They are also amazingly good at tracking their prey through the oceans. They have super-sharp senses, and can detect the scent of blood in the water from more than half a mile (800 meters) away. So when you go out on your shark-diving trip, you trail a bag of meat and dead fish from the dive

Powerful hunters like tuna and dolphins are near the top of the ocean **food chain.** But even they have enemies. The **predators** at the very top of the food chain include some of the most efficient killers on Earth—sharks.

The most feared of all sharks is the great white shark. It can grow to more than 20 feet (6 meters) long, and it has huge, razor-edged triangular teeth. Unlike most sharks, it feeds mainly on warm-blooded animals like seals and dolphins. It also eats big, meaty fish such as tuna. A great white shark can slice a seal in half with a single bite, and could easily do the same to you. So be careful, because you are going to meet one!

Super senses

The great white shark lives mainly in cool coastal waters, and avoids the **tropical** oceans. To find one, you travel south to

Great white sharks look very scary, and their teeth can cut through skin and bone. But these sharks rarely kill people.

boat to attract sharks. Then the crew hang a shark cage over the side. You put on your scuba gear, lower yourself into the cage, and wait.

Waiting for a shark

At first nothing happens. A few small fish appear and nibble at the bait, but no sharks. You start to relax. But then there is a thump from behind, and the cage lurches in the water. You turn around to see a scary set of teeth biting at the steel cage, only inches from your face. You are knocked to the other side of the cage as the shark bangs into it. The shark loses some teeth, which fall through the water. You will remember this for a long time.

Shark cage

A shark cage is made of thick steel bars that even a great white shark cannot bite through. There is a gap in the bars so that divers can use underwater cameras to film or photograph the sharks. The gap is too small for a shark to get through.

A Cool Ocean Current

The Cape fur seals of South Africa feed in an area of ocean to the west of Cape Town. The water here is affected by a flow of cool water called the Benguela Current. It flows north from the icy Antarctic Ocean, up the southwest coast of Africa toward the **equator.** The **current** has an important effect on the ocean wildlife, as you soon discover.

Cape fur seals spend much of their time swimming underwater in the sunlit zone. Here, they feed on fish.

Heading north from Cape Town, you stop off in southern Namibia and hire a fast shark-fishing boat. As your driver speeds west, away from the coast, you drag a heat sensor in the water.

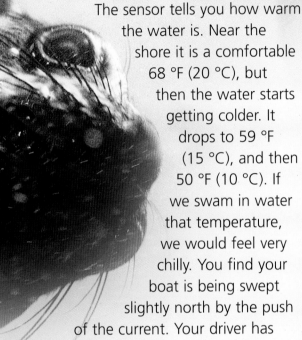

copepod

krill

These tiny creatures (right) have been magnified by a microscope. Some are shrimplike krill. The others are copepods. They form part of the plankton in the cool waters of the Benguela Current.

The sensor tells you how warm the water is. Near the shore it is a comfortable 68 °F (20 °C), but then the water starts getting colder. It drops to 59 °F (15 °C), and then 50 °F (10 °C). If we swam in water that temperature, we would feel very chilly. You find your boat is being swept slightly north by the push of the current. Your driver has to steer to the southeast. Otherwise you would be pushed off course. You are crossing the Benguela Current.

After you have traveled for two hours, the water starts warming up again. You also notice it has changed color, from green to blue. You stop the boat and dive over the side. The water is crystal clear, and you can see a long way underwater. But there are few fish to look at. You gather a water sample, then turn the boat around and head back toward the coast.

Green ocean

The sea turns green again as you start to enter the cold current. You dive back in for a look. It is colder and cloudier. As you climb back on board you notice some seabirds diving for fish. You scan the horizon with your binoculars. There are many birds over the green ocean to the east, but few to the west, where it is blue.

You take another water sample and check it with a hand-held **microscope.** The water is full of **plankton.** Yet the blue-water sample has hardly any plankton. This explains why the cool green water is attracting so many fish and birds.

Ocean upwelling

The ocean off the coast of Namibia is full of life. The combination of the wind and Earth's rotation drags the surface water away from the coast. Deep, **nutrient**-rich water is drawn up from the ocean floor to take its place. The result is an **upwelling zone.** The ocean in the upwelling zone is thick with plankton. Huge shoals of fish live there, too. They eat the plankton. The zone is one of the best fishing grounds in Africa.

Feeding Frenzy

You have already learned a lot from looking at ocean **plankton.** You have found that tiny plantlike **algae** make food by **photosynthesis.** Algae are eaten, in turn, by **microscopic** animals. Algae and the small animals that eat them are scooped up by bigger animals, including flying fish, whale sharks, and manta rays. And hunters like frigatebirds eat some of the fish. Together they form a food web (lots of linked **food chains**). All the animals in the sunlit zone depend on food made by the algae.

To see the oceanic food web in action, you travel north in the Benguela Current, just off the coast of Namibia. This is an **upwelling zone.** There, cold water is being drawn up from the ocean floor, bringing **nutrients** with it. The algae near the surface use these nutrients to grow and multiply. The more nutrients and sunshine, the faster the algae multiply. There is more food for animals of all kinds—from shrimp to sharks—in upwelling areas.

Millions of tuna fish are caught in nets by fishers for people to eat. But these fish are also hunters themselves. They hunt and eat smaller fish.

Mass attack

The clouds of algae feed swarms of animal plankton, such as copepods. These are eaten by huge shoals of small plankton-feeding fish, such as sardines, herrings, and anchovies. And the fish attract hungry hunters like tuna, seabirds, and dolphins. Tuna are big, powerful, fast-swimming killers. They hunt in groups called schools. When tuna find a shoal of smaller fish, such as herring, they surge in to attack. The herring defend themselves by forming a tight, swirling ball of fast-swimming fish. The tuna try to break up the ball, so they can pick off the fish one by one.

Watching from a boat, you see the herring leaping out of the water as they try to escape. The water looks as though it is boiling. And you are not the only one watching. Seabirds are always on the lookout for the chance to eat. Some, called gannets, have spotted the fuss. They swoop from the sky, diving into the water to seize the fish in their beaks. A school of dolphins joins the feast. Some of the dolphins circle the fish to keep them in place. Others take turns to swim through the shoal and feed. It is a feeding frenzy.

Water and Weather

During your trip back across the Benguela Current, you operate a weather station to keep track of any changes in the weather. Not surprisingly, your **thermometer** shows a drop in air temperature above the cool **current.** The **hygrometer** also shows that the air is very humid, or full of moisture. But you can tell this, anyway, because the boat has run into a thick bank of fog.

Fog at sea can be dangerous, because your boat could be hit by another ship. So the captain starts sounding the foghorn to warn other ships. He also switches on the boat's **radar.** This sends out radio signals that reflect, or bounce back, off any solid objects. The radar set picks up the echo, and shows the position of the object on a screen. By watching the radar screen, you can avoid other ships and find your way safely through the fog.

But why is it so foggy? The weather station gives a clue. The Sun makes water **evaporate** (turn to vapor) from the ocean and rise up into the air. So the air above any ocean has water vapor in it. But if the air is cooled by contact with colder water, the vapor **condenses** and turns to fog. It may even turn to rain. Eventually rain can remove much moisture from the air.

Usually, air blowing off the ocean contains some moisture. This often falls on the land as rain. But any air that moves east over the cold Benguela Current loses nearly all its moisture at sea before it reaches the coast of Namibia. Some fog may reach the land, but no rain. So the whole coastal region of Namibia is a bone-dry desert, created by an ocean current.

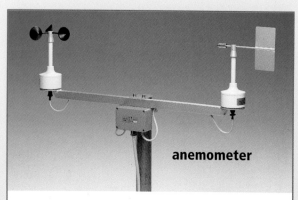

anemometer

Weather station

Your mini-weather station contains:
- an anemometer for measuring the speed of the wind;
- a thermometer for measuring temperature;
- a hygrometer for measuring humidity; and
- a barometer for measuring air pressure.

This photograph has been taken from a satellite very high above Earth. The brown areas are land (the Namib Desert). The dark blue areas are the South Atlantic Ocean. And the fluffy white patches are fog over the cool Benguela Current.

Walvis Bay

AFRICA

Namib Desert

Namibia

Namib Desert

Blue and green patches show where water is rising from the ocean bottom.

Fog and cloud over cool Benguela Current.

The Weedy Sargasso Sea

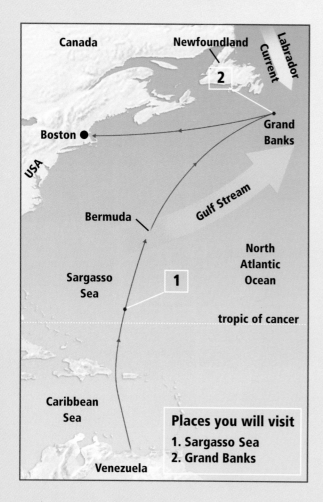

Canada
Newfoundland
Labrador Current
2
Grand Banks
Boston
USA
Gulf Stream
Bermuda
North Atlantic Ocean
Sargasso Sea
1
tropic of cancer
Caribbean Sea

Places you will visit
1. Sargasso Sea
2. Grand Banks

Venezuela

The Benguela Current is part of a great swirl of ocean **currents** called a **gyre.** The gyre flows counterclockwise around the South Atlantic. There is a similar gyre in the North Atlantic, which flows clockwise. Both gyres meet and flow westward at the **equator.**

In the middle of each gyre is a calm area of ocean. There is little wind, and the sea is usually calm. A calm area inside the North

Atlantic gyre is called the Sargasso Sea. That will be your next destination.

Floating hazard

You get there on a big sailing yacht that is heading from Venezuela to Bermuda. At first the journey goes well. The winds that help drive the ocean currents fill the sails and drive the yacht through the water. They are called the trade winds, because trading ships used them to cross oceans when all ships traveled by sail.

As you cross the **tropic of cancer** the winds start to die away. You are entering the calm zone. The old sailing ships avoided this region because there was not enough wind to fill their sails and blow them along. But your boat has an engine so you can keep going into the Sargasso Sea. Your instruments show that there is hardly any current, and the sea is warm, very salty, and crystal clear. There is little or no **plankton** in the water.

Sargassum weed

Suddenly you hit trouble. A great mass of brown seaweed has wrapped itself around the yacht's propeller. Looking around, you

can see more seaweed. It is sargassum weed. Sargassum weed floats in huge mats on the surface. One of the crew dives over the side with a knife to free the propeller. You dive overboard, too, to take a closer look at the seaweed. Hiding in the sargassum weed are strange creatures that live nowhere else on Earth. One is the

This sargassum fish looks like the weed where it lives. This helps hide the fish from bigger fish that may eat it.

sargassum fish. It takes you a long time to find one of these fish. When you do, you see why: it looks very much like the seaweed it lives in.

Exploring the Gulf Stream

At Bermuda you join an ocean research ship from the Marine Biological Laboratory at Woods Hole, Massachusetts. The ship is heading into the Gulf Stream. The Gulf Stream is a warm **current** coming from the **equator,** the Gulf of Mexico, and Florida. It warms the **climate** of the northeastern United States, Iceland, and the British Isles. In winter, western Europe is much milder than eastern Canada, even though both are the same distance from the equator.

The Gulf Stream is a powerful current. It flows about as fast as you can walk if you are in a hurry. Every second it moves enough water to fill 5 billion buckets. Its speed makes the current very useful to anything headed in the same direction, including ships and ocean animals.

Turtle trail

One of the animals that tags along for the ride is the giant leatherback turtle. This ocean giant grows up to 6 feet (1.8 meters) long. That is as long as a man is tall. Leatherback turtles feed mainly on jellyfish. To find jellyfish, leatherbacks swim hundreds or sometimes thousands of miles into the North Atlantic, riding the Gulf Stream.

Leatherbacks are becoming fewer and fewer. They are in danger of dying out completely. The crew of the research ship wants to track the leatherbacks on their travels. After a day following the Gulf Stream, the pilot of the ship's small plane spots a leatherback swimming near the surface. You decide to take a closer look using the ship's **submersible.**

Seeing with sound

The submersible has an underwater **sonar** system, which uses sound signals to locate things underwater. The sonar soon finds the turtle, and before long you can see it through the clear blue water. The turtle is swimming powerfully, using its huge

Leatherback turtles are the biggest turtles that swim in the sea. They can dive right to the bottom of the sunlit zone.

A submersible is lowered over the side of a research ship. Submersibles can dive to very great depths.

flippers like wings. The turtle is following a crowd of jellyfish. You follow in the submersible. The tentacles hanging from the jellyfish can sting, but you are safe inside the submersible. The turtle does not seem to notice, and snaps up four or five jellyfish with its beaklike mouth. It will stay with the jellyfish swarm until it has eaten many of them.

Submersible

A submersible is a small submarine used for scientific research. Many submersibles are designed to dive very deep. They have very thick windows to resist the strong **water pressure** in the deep ocean. Submersibles have lights, cameras, and mechanical arms for collecting samples from the water and the seabed.

Rich Fishing

The research ship you are traveling on heads northeast in the Gulf Stream. Eventually, off the coast of eastern Canada, you get to the Grand Banks. There, the ship meets another great ocean **current.** This is the cold Labrador Current, which flows south from the Arctic Ocean.

The Labrador Current carries a lot of **nutrients,** just like the Benguela Current in the South Atlantic. The cold waters of the Labrador Current mix with the warm water of the Gulf Stream. The combination of the Labrador Current's nutrients and lots of summer sunshine make the **algae** in the **plankton** grow. The result is a very rich sea, full of plankton and fish.

Algae need light and nutrients to multiply. Since this area lies so far north, there is not much daylight in winter. But all that changes in spring. Then, long hours of daylight cause an explosion of plankton growth. Since you get to the Grand Banks in early May, you arrive in the middle of a **plankton bloom.**

A fishing trip

The research ship has to stop off at Newfoundland. You decide to change boats and join a fishing boat on a trip out over the Grand Banks. The Grand Banks is an area off the coast of Newfoundland. You notice that the sea is green with **microscopic** life. Everywhere there are seabirds feeding on and in the water. There is obviously a lot of food here.

Gannets dive into the ocean from as high as an apartment building 60 feet (18 meters) tall. The bird grabs fish with its beak.

A fisher dumps a haul of large crabs on the deck of a Grand Banks trawler.

The seabed is about 500 feet (150 meters) below the surface. It is a flooded part of the North American continent called the **continental shelf.** It is not nearly as deep as the ocean floor in most places. Since the ocean here is relatively shallow, fishing boats can catch big bottom-feeding fish such as skates and flounders. But the area has been heavily fished for many years, and these fish are getting scarce. Fishing for cod and flounders over the Grand Banks is now controlled. The crew on the boat you are on are fishing for crabs instead.

A big surprise

While the crew haul up their catch of crabs, you watch some big white seabirds called gannets **plunge-diving** to catch fish in their long beaks. Meanwhile, much bigger animals are moving in from the ocean for their share. One of them suddenly leaps from the water not far away: a giant humpback whale!

Whale Watch

When the fishing boat gets back to Newfoundland you rejoin the research ship. It is heading back to its home port near Boston. On the way, you want to use the ship's **submersible** to watch humpback whales.

Every year the whales move from **tropical** seas to cooler northern waters to feast on fish during the spring **plankton bloom.** They are huge animals, up to 60 feet (18 meters) long. That's longer than a school bus. They have very long flippers. In places where there is plenty of food, they gather in groups of 20 or more. They often work as a team to round up and catch fish.

As the ship moves south, you carefully watch the ocean. You are soon rewarded by the sight of a huge black shape lunging up from the water. It is the snout of a humpback whale. Its throat is stretched into a huge bag full of water. And there is water pouring from the edges of its mouth.

Two adult humpback whales leap out of the water. This behavior is called breaching.

A humpback feeds by gulping enormous mouthfuls of water, fish, and **plankton.** The whale then squeezes the water out through rows of platelike structures called baleen plates. The edges of the plates form a fringe around the whale's mouth. The plates keep the food from escaping with the water. Many other very large whales also have baleen instead of teeth.

Bubble netting

When you are lowered over the side in the submersible, you cannot see far because the water is cloudy with plankton. But as you move away from the ship, you start hearing strange noises. Your **sonar** shows that there are whales all around you. Then you see a great dark shape. You ask the driver of the submersible to steer toward the shape so you can get a better view.

The humpback whale is swimming around a shoal of herring, blowing bubbles of air from its mouth. The bubbles rise through the water. They form a silvery net around the shoal of fish. The whale is doing this on purpose. The **bubble net** makes the shoal bunch together in a tight ball. When the fish are packed very tightly, the whale swims up and scoops thousands of them into its mouth. The whale's behavior is called bubble netting.

A Red Tide

The western North Atlantic, near Canada and New England, contains large amounts of **plankton** for most of the year. This is usually good news for ocean wildlife. But sometimes there can be too much plankton.

In places, the surface water of the western Atlantic is pushed toward the shore. To escape, it flows downward when it runs close to the coast. The result is called a **downwelling zone.** As the water moves toward the shore, it carries large amounts of plankton with it. But the plankton floats and does not sink with the downflow. It stays at the surface, where it is joined by more plankton drawn in from the ocean. The plankton gets thicker and thicker, and changes the color of the water. The water may turn pink, violet, orange, yellow, blue, green, or red. Red is the most common color, so blooms of plankton are often called red tides.

Back to Boston

As your ship heads back to its home port near Boston, it sails through a large area where the water is rusty red. You take samples of the plankton and check them under a **microscope.** They are **algae** called dinoflagellates. They look harmless, but if there are enough of them, they can kill.

Some types of dinoflagellate produce tiny amounts of poison. Usually, this does not matter. However, sometimes the type of

---

When dinoflagellates collect in huge numbers, they can make the water change color. Sometimes they color the ocean red. This is called a red tide.

Microscope

Many types of plankton are too small to see without a microscope. The microscope on your research ship magnifies things 20 times. It has an eyepiece for each eye. You can see the plankton lit up against a dark background by a lighting system.

plankton that blooms releases a poison that can be deadly to fish, seabirds, and other animals. Red tides off Florida have killed millions of fish, which often get washed up on beaches

In 1977, a re____
New Jersey m____
large area of the____
could swim away ____
those that could n____
numbers of fish—die____

Another problem is that ____ ____ umbers of plankton in the water e____ y use up the **nutrient** supply. Then, a____ plankton dies. The dead plankton are e___en by bacteria, which multiply and use up all the oxygen in the water. Fish cannot live without oxygen, so they die, too.

The Frozen Ocean

North Pole

Part of Arctic Ocean that is frozen all year.

dive site

Greenland

Part of Arctic Ocean that is frozen in winter.

Murmansk

Russia

An icebreaker ship is designed to cut channels through sea ice. It slices straight through thin ice. It is powerful enough to ride up on top of thicker ice and smash it by sheer weight. It can break solid ice that is more than 3 feet (1 meter) thick.

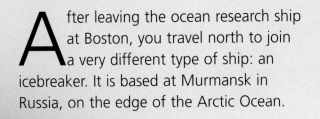

After leaving the ocean research ship at Boston, you travel north to join a very different type of ship: an icebreaker. It is based at Murmansk in Russia, on the edge of the Arctic Ocean.

More than half of the Arctic Ocean is always covered in ice. Much of the sunlit zone there is frozen. Even the North Pole is just a point on the ice-covered ocean. Most of this **sea ice** is about 10 feet (3 meters) thick—at least twice as thick as you are tall. The polar ice never melts, but the sea ice around the fringes melts each summer and freezes again in winter. It is the icebreaker's job to cut channels through the thinner ice.

When you arrive in late May, most of the ocean is still iced over. The icebreaker is out at sea clearing a channel, but a helicopter comes to fetch you. The flight takes you north over open water to the sea ice. The sea ice covers the ocean in a glittering white sheet. You see the black and cream icebreaker below, moving south through the ice and leaving a dark ribbon of open water behind it.

Crunching ice

When you get on board, you take some samples of the ocean water. It is hard to see how anything could survive in it, but you discover a lot of **plankton.** As the icebreaker crunches its way toward open water, your samples show even more plankton. Many seabirds are diving for fish. The ocean is obviously full of life.

The cold water is full of **nutrients** stirred up from the ocean floor by deepwater **currents.** But the **algae** in the plankton cannot grow during the Arctic winter. They need sunlight to grow, and the Arctic is always dark in winter. When spring arrives, the darkness gives way to 24-hour daylight. The air gets warmer, and the ice at the ocean surface starts to melt. There is a massive bloom of plankton. And there is also plenty of food for all kinds of animals.

Diving with Seals

One way to see what lives in the icy Arctic Ocean is to dive below the ice edge and look. You decide to do just that, wearing **scuba** gear and a thermal **drysuit** to keep you warm.

The scene below is bathed in a beautiful blue light glowing through the ice. Your suit works so well that you cannot feel the cold. But the other animals that live here do not need special suits. You follow some Arctic cod, which are feeding on **plankton** animals. Even though these fish are near freezing point, they are able to survive. This is because chemicals in their bodies keep them from freezing.

Then something swoops past you and chases after the cod. It is a ringed seal. The seal can swim fast because its body is streamlined. It is covered with a thick layer of fat called blubber. The blubber also works as **insulation.** The insulation stops the seal's body heat from draining into the near-frozen water. Other warm-blooded animals that live in the Arctic Ocean, such as whales and white-sided dolphins, keep warm in the same way.

Under the ice

You follow the seal under the ice for a few minutes while it chases and catches fish. But soon it has to rise to the surface to breathe. It heads for a hole in the ice and swims up into the daylight.

You are about to follow when you hear a muffled thump. The ice around the hole bursts apart and the great front paws of a polar bear punch down through the water. The bear seizes the seal in its jaws and pulls it on to the ice, leaving a trail of blood. You slip away quickly, back to open water. Maybe it is time to go home.

Keeping warm

Without a drysuit you would soon freeze to death in the water of the Arctic Ocean, because the water temperature is a very cold 32 °F (0 °C). Fresh water freezes at this temperature, but salty seawater freezes at the lower temperature of 29 °F (−1.8 °C). Your drysuit is made of rubber that keeps heat from escaping from your body. So the suit keeps you warm and safe.

A harp seal pokes its head out of a hole in the ice. Seals breathe air, like we do, so they need to come to the surface to fill their lungs. You can tell it is very cold—this seal has ice on its whiskers.

Mission Debriefing

You have discovered a lot on your journey through the sunlit zone. Before you started, you might have thought that the warmest oceans were the ones with most life. Your trip to the **coral reef** certainly made it look that way. But, away from land, many warm **tropical** oceans do not have that many creatures living in them.

The things that bring an ocean to life are **nutrients** and sunlight. The nutrients are stirred up by ocean **currents.** They are absorbed by the **microscopic algae** in the **plankton,** which use sunlight to make food. The algae then grow and multiply and are eaten by tiny **plankton** animals. The plankton provides food for fish and all the other animals in the ocean. In some places, this happens all year round. In other places the plankton supply varies with the seasons.

Ocean currents also carry warm water toward the poles and cold water toward the tropics. They make Earth a more comfortable place to live, especially in places like western Europe. But ocean currents can also create deserts, like the Namib Desert in southwest Africa. So the oceans affect us all, wherever we live.

Plankton such as these radiolarians are eaten by bigger creatures in the sunlit zone.

Glossary

absorb soak up

algae plantlike living things. Some are tiny, single cells. Others can be very big, like some seaweeds.

bubble net "net" of bubbles blown by a whale and designed to scare or confuse fish and make them easier to catch

climate weather of a place over a year

clones two or more living things that have exactly the same chemical makeup

cold-blooded animal whose body temperature is controlled by the temperature of the air or water around it

colony group of living things that live together in the same place

condense when a gas cools and becomes a liquid

continental shelf gently sloping edge of a continent, covered by a shallow sea

coral reef structure built by a large group of corals with chalky skeletons. Corals are small, sea anemone-like animals.

current flow of ocean water

downwelling zone area of the ocean where ocean currents drag the surface water downward. It is often near a coast.

drysuit waterproof clothing that keeps a diver dry and warm in the ocean

egg living cell produced by a female organism

equator imaginary line around the center of Earth, halfway between the North and South Poles

evaporate turn to vapor, or gas. When water turns to steam, it has evaporated.

fertilize when a male sex cell (sperm) joins with a female sex cell (egg) to begin the development of a young organism

food chain organization of animals and plants that shows who eats what

gene part of a cell in all living things. Genes are passed from adult animals to their young. They control how the young organisms look and grow.

gills parts of a fish's body through which it breathes

gyre big swirl of water currents that revolves around an entire ocean

hygrometer instrument that measures how damp the air is

insulation anything that stops heat passing from one place to another. An animal's fat or fur is insulation.

lagoon shallow area of ocean enclosed by a coral reef

limestone hard rock made from the remains of shells or chalky coral skeletons

microscope device for looking at things too small to see with the naked eye

microscopic things that are too small to see with the naked eye

nutrients substances that are needed by animals and plants to stay strong and healthy. Proteins, minerals, and vitamins are all nutrients.

organisms living things. All plants, algae, and animals are organisms.

photosynthesis process by which organisms use sunlight to turn chemicals into energy

plankton animals, plants, and plantlike organisms, including algae, that drift near the surface of the ocean

plankton bloom very large increase in the number of animals, plants, and plantlike organisms drifting in the ocean

plunge-diving fishing technique used by seabirds, such as gannets, that dive straight into the sea

predators animals that hunt, kill, and eat other animals

radar device that locates things by bouncing radio signals off them

reef slope outer edge of a coral reef, which slopes steeply down into deep water

scuba equipment that divers use so that they can breathe under water

sea ice frozen part of the sunlit zone. Sea ice covers most of Arctic Ocean and the edges of Antarctica.

sonar device that locates things by bouncing sound signals off them

spawn release male and female sex cells into the water

sperm male sex cell

submersible a small submarine designed for short trips. Some can dive to great depths.

thermometer instrument that measures temperature

tropical of the tropics. The tropics are the hot parts of Earth either side of the equator.

tropic of cancer northern border of the tropical part of Earth

upwelling zone area of the ocean where ocean currents drag the water up from the ocean floor

water pressure force of water pressing down on something

water vapor gas formed when water is heated

Further Reading and Websites

Books

Byatt, Andrew, *et. al. Blue Planet.* New York: DK Publishing, 2002.

Day, Trevor. *Oceans and Beaches.* Austin, Tex.: Raintree/Steck-Vaughn, 2003.

Green, Jen. *A Coral Reef.* New York: Crabtree, 2000.

Laskey, Elizabeth. *Seahorses.* Chicago: Heinemann Library, 2003.

Theodorou, Rod. *Inside a Coral Reef.* Chicago: Heinemann Library, 1998.

Websites

www.bbc.co.uk/nature/blueplanet
The website of the BBC series about ocean life, with extra information and games.

oceanexplorer.noaa.gov
The website of the U.S. National Oceanic and Atmospheric Administration, about the technology of ocean exploration and ocean wildlife.

www.seasky.org/sea.html
A website packed with information about the ocean.

www.underwaterphotography.com/articles/travel/palau.asp
A virtual tour of the undersea world around the Rock Islands of Palau.

Index

ML

/05

ML